How to Art Doodle™ Fabulous Things!

Carolyn Scrace

This edition first published in MMXV by
Book House

Distributed by Black Rabbit Books
P.O. Box 3263
Mankato
Minnesota MN 56002

© MMXV The Salariya Book Company Ltd
Printed in the United States of America.
Printed on paper from sustainable forests.

Cataloging-in-Publication Data is available
from the Library of Congress

HB ISBN: 978-1-909645-46-2
PB ISBN: 978-1-910184-34-9

How to Art Doodle Fabulous Things!

Carolyn Scrace

BOOK HOUSE

Contents

5   Introduction

6   Art Doodling on objects

8   Tools & materials

10   Pebble animals

12   Monster T-shirt!

14   Doodled jars

16   Crazy collage

18   Arty carton

20   Origami bird

22   Pattern builder

23   Glossary

24   Index

Please note: Sharp blades and scissors should be used under adult supervision.

Introduction

Discover the thrill of transforming mundane objects into exciting works of art! Have fun experimenting with different techniques and using a variety of materials to doodle. Art Doodling develops drawing and design skills and encourages creativity.

Interesting objects

Keep a collection of interesting objects to Art Doodle, such as stones, shells, driftwood, bottles, containers, old clothes, and china. There are endless opportunities to embellish and decorate them.

Inspiration

Inspiration is all around you—even in the most surprising places! Carry a small sketchbook with you to capture any patterns and ideas. Stick in any magazine cuttings that inspire or excite you, and remember to use your sketchbook as work in progress!

Creative confidence

As your creative confidence grows, your skills and ability as an artist will increase too, enabling you to design and develop your own personal style of Art Doodling.

Art Doodling on objects

Wherever you look there are objects simply waiting to be Art Doodled! Glass, cardboard, paper, fabric, stone, leaves, shells—the list of surfaces is endless. Doodling around three-dimensional shapes, whether curved, flat, rounded, or angular, can be challenging—but the results are both exciting and surprising. Use this book as a springboard into the world of Art Doodling fabulous things!

Doodling leaves

Fallen leaves are great objects to doodle. Choose firm, waxy leaves with a simple shape. Experiment with different pens to find out which makes the best lines on the surface of the leaf. As a rule, white, gold, and silver gel pens are best for doodling on dark colors and black fineliner pens are great for doodling on pale colors.

Doodling shells and pebbles

An abandoned snail shell is a terrifically inspiring shape to Art Doodle. Use simple, bold patterns to follow the spiraling curve of the shell. Black fineliner and gold gel pens work well against this pale-colored background.

See pages 10–11 to learn how to Art Doodle pebbles.

Doodling cardboard tubes

A fantastic way to experiment with doodling on curved surfaces is to use the cardboard tube from a kitchen roll. Cut the tube in half and have fun trying out different patterns. Wacky faces make a fun theme to try first!

Pencil in the main shapes of the face. Go over the lines with black, permanent marker pen. Block in areas of color with felt-tips. Now start Art Doodling patterns. Try white, silver, and gold gel pens to doodle on darker tones and black and dark-colored gel pens on lighter areas.

7

Pencil sharpener

Eraser

Thick **marker pens** are perfect for filling in large areas. Fine **permanent marker** pens are great for outlines and details.

Graphite pencils come in different grades, from hard to soft.

Tools & materials

There are no special tools and materials needed for Art Doodling fabulous things. A felt-tip pen and some old packaging is all you need to get started. You may, however, wish to use some or all of the tools and materials suggested here. It's important to experiment as some materials work better on certain surfaces than others.

Pencil crayons are ideal for adding soft shading to an area. Use them for coloring in.

Felt-tip pens come in a range of thicknesses. Thick pens are ideal for blocking-in large areas of color.

Fineliner pens produce a flowing line and are ideal for intricate doodling. They come in a wide range of colors which creates added appeal.

A black gel pen is useful for outlines and detailed doodles. **Metallic and white gel pens** make the ideal choice for doodling onto darker colors.

Sequins

Double-sided tape

Sketchbook for jotting down ideas and trying out designs.

Use your sketchbook to experiment with new techniques and to keep notes of which materials were used.

Permanent fabric markers for drawing on cotton clothing. Air dry or iron to make the colors permanent.

Types of paper

Cartridge paper comes in a variety of thicknesses. Heavyweight paper is good for water-based paint. Note: Ink lines may bleed (run) on some cartridge papers.

Bristol board or **paper** may be textured or smooth. Smooth Bristol board is good to work on with pencils, pencil crayons, markers, felt-tips, and gel and fineliner pens for adding fine details.

Origami paper comes in a variety of thicknesses and finishes. Other types of paper (for example printing paper) can be used, provided they can be folded and creased.

Palette (or clean saucer) for mixing paint.

Paintbrushes come in a wide range of sizes.

Colored inks and **watercolor** paints are ideal for covering large areas of a design with subtle color.

White acrylic primer is fast-drying and opaque. It produces a surface that is good for painting or doodling on.

Gouache is opaque watercolor. Use it for painting plain, flat areas.

Pebble animals

Smooth stones and pebbles are fantastic shapes to Art Doodle. Try using the theme of animals to inspire your designs. Choose a selection of differently shaped stones to Art Doodle.

1. Roughly sketch in the pebble outline then draw an animal inspired by its shape. Try out some Art Doodles.

2. Pencil the main shapes of your design onto the pebble.

3. Go over the pencil lines using a black fineliner and fine felt-tip pens.

4. Use white gel pen for the eye. Use delicate lines to add art doodle patterns.

These cat and owl designs were used to decorate the pebbles shown opposite.

Use gold and silver gel pens to highlight areas such as the cat's ears, heart-shaped chest, and paws.

See page 22 for a step-by-step guide to creating the feather pattern used to Art Doodle the owl.

Using a bold, black zig-zag pattern around the edges makes the rabbit shape stand out.

Monster T-shirt!

Customize your T-shirt with a friendly Art Doodled monster!

You will need:
White or pale-colored T-shirt
Permanent fabric markers
Large sheets of paper
Cardboard
Pencil
Colored crayon
Sticky tape
Scissors
Black felt-tip pen

1. Start by making a rough sketch of your design on scrap paper. **Artist's tip:** Drawing the monster at an angle creates a more dynamic composition!

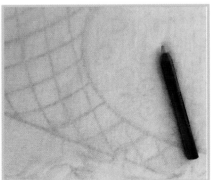

2. Trace the T-shirt shape onto A3 paper (or tape sheets together). Now pencil in your design and go over the lines with black felt-tip pen.

3. Cut out the paper shape and lay it inside the T-shirt on top of the cardboard. Use a yellow pencil crayon to trace the lines. Remove the paper.

4. Go over the lines with black fabric marker. Consider the tonal balance of your patterns; contrast pale yellow curls with dark black scales.

See page 22 for a doodle guide to this scale pattern.

Artist's tip: use a limited palette of colors for a "sophisticated" looking monster!

5. Follow the manufacturer's instructions to "fix" the fabric marker pen lines.

Doodled jars

O ld jars are ready-made objects just waiting to be adorned with creative Art Doodling! Use them as personalized storage vessels or vases!

You will need:

Assorted, clean glass jars
Artist's white acrylic primer
Large paintbrush
Permanent markers
Metallic fine-pointed, permanent markers
Paper kitchen towels
Raffia
Clear varnish (optional)

1. Protect your work surface with paper towels. Paint the outsides of the jars using acrylic primer and leave to dry.

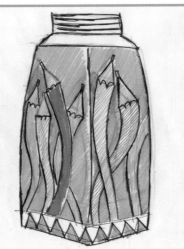

2. Make color roughs of your ideas, using bold, simple designs.

3. Use black marker to draw in the main elements of the design. Start blocking in areas of color.

4. Leave a thin white border around the main shapes then color in the background. Art Doodle silver, marker pen dots, and a zig-zag border.

The design (below left) was inspired by a fairytale princess!

Experiment! Try leaving areas of clear glass when painting on primer. Then doodle around the edges (see above).

Note: If permanent markers have been used, the finished designs can be coated with clear varnish.

5. As a finishing touch wind raffia around the screw top, tie securely, then trim the ends.

15

Crazy collage

A collage is a picture composed of different materials stuck down onto a background. This collage uses steampunk as its theme and combines magazine cuttings with Art Doodling, sequins, buttons, beads, and old keys!

You will need:
Old magazines
Double-sided tape
Cartridge paper
Sequins
Buttons
Beads
Scissors
Felt-tip pens
Fineliner pens
PVA glue

1. Use magazine cuttings of faces and arms to stick onto cartridge paper (as shown). Draw in the shoulders.

2. Sketch in steampunk goggles, then complete the shape of the head with a series of drawings of cogs, wheels, nuts, and bolts!

3. Draw in a huge moustache, a hat brim, and a watch and chain. Block in areas with gold, gray, and black felt-tips. Use fineliner pens for fine Art Doodles.

4. Glue a selection of sequins, old buttons, and beads onto your artwork. Old keys add an air of mystery to this collage.

Arty carton

Even the most ordinary carton or box can be transformed into a fabulous, doodled work of art!

1. Make thumbnail sketches of your ideas. This snake design winds around the carton.

2. Cut the tracing paper to wrap round the carton. Draw your design on it.

3. Trace your finished design onto cartridge paper and cut to fit. Tape it around the carton.

18

4. Now have fun Art Doodling! Use black, white, and gray doodles. Focus attention on specific areas by using spots of bright red pattern.

See page 22 for a guide to creating the pattern on the snake's body.

Artist's tip: Highlight points of interest such as a beetle, butterfly, flowers, and the snake's head to ensure the design works from all viewpoints.

5. Add shading beneath the snake's body to make it stand out from the rest of the design.

Origami bird

You will need:
Square sheet of thin paper for folding

1. Fold in half, crease, and unfold.

2. Fold along dotted lines so corners meet on center line.

3. Fold top backward along the dotted line.

4. Fold inward along the dotted line, then crease.

5. Pull the inside part outward.

6. Fold flat as shown. Repeat on opposite side.

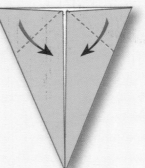

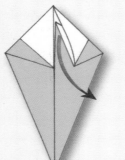

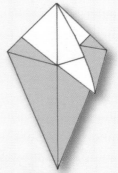

7. Repeat steps **5–6** on the other side.

8. Fold upward along the dotted lines.

9. Make a zig-zag fold along the dotted lines, then crease.

10. Fold tail inward, then crease.

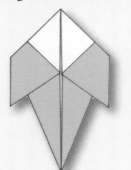

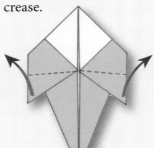

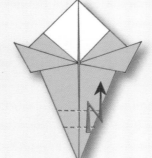

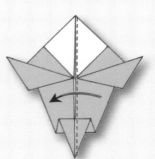

11. Turn sideways.

12. Make a pocket fold along the dotted line.

Now have fun Art Doodling!

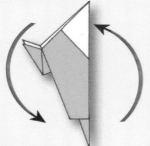

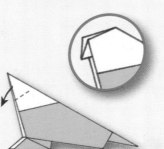

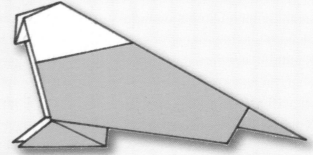

Origami is the traditional Japanese art of folding squares of paper to create shapes representing animals and flowers.

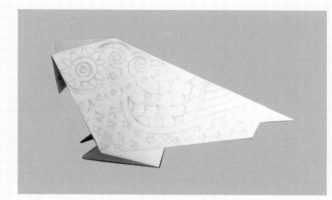

1. Pencil in the bird's eye and wing. Now draw in the main doodle shapes.

2. Unfold the origami bird and lay it flat before you doodle it. Use fineliner, gel, and felt-tip pens.

21

Pattern builder

These step-by-step examples show how to Art Doodle some of the patterns used in this book.

Pebble animals... the owl (Pages 10-11)

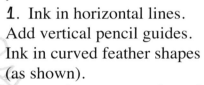

1. Ink in horizontal lines. Add vertical pencil guides. Ink in curved feather shapes (as shown).

2. Ink in a vertical line to represent the shaft of each feather and add rows of angled lines (as shown).

3. Add more curved lines to create thick borders and fill in with black fineliner.

Monster T-shirt (Pages 12-13)

1. Pencil in a grid. Draw in diagonal lines in both directions (as shown).

2. Draw small semi-circles at the top of each diamond shape. Fill in as solid black.

3. Add small curved lines. Fill in the shape at the base of each diamond shape.

Arty carton... the snake (Pages 18-19)

1. Ink in horizontal lines. Draw two zig-zag lines and fill with circles (as shown).

2. Draw smaller versions above. Fill the lower triangles with alternating angled lines.

3. Fill the base with short vertical lines to represent the snake's underbelly.

Glossary

Background area behind an object or image.

Blocking in where areas of flat color are put down.

Collage a technique for making a work of art by sticking pieces of different materials such as paper, cloth, or wood onto a flat surface.

Color rough a quick sketch of the principal colored elements in a picture.

Composition how an artist arranges shapes, sizes, and colors, the different elements that make a piece of art.

Customize to modify or change the appearance of an item to suit an individual.

Design a graphic representation, usually a drawing or a sketch.

Dynamic concerned with energy or motion.

Embellish to improve or make beautiful by adding detail or ornament.

Intensity a measurement of the difference between a color and pure grey.

Layout an arrangement, plan, or design.

Limited palette when an artist restricts the number of colors used.

Origami the Japanese art or process of folding paper into recognizable shapes.

Raffia a fibre used for tying, weaving, etc.

Rough a quick sketch of the main elements in a picture.

Sequins a small piece of shiny metal foil or plastic used to decorate fabric.

Sketch a preparatory drawing.

Steampunk a type of fantasy art, featuring machines and other technology, based on steam power of the 19th century.

Technique an accepted method used to produce something.

Three dimensions having, or appearing to have, the dimension of depth as well as width and height.

Thumbnail (sketches) usually small, quick, abbreviated drawings.

Index

A

acrylic primer   9, 14

B

background   7, 14, 16
border   14
Bristol board   9

C

cardboard   7, 12, 18
cartridge paper   9, 18
collage   16, 17
color rough   12
composition   12, 23

D

design   5, 10, 18, 19

F

felt-tip pen   7, 8, 12, 16
fineliner pen   6, 7, 8, 10, 16, 21

G

gel pen   7, 8, 10, 21

H

highlight   11

J

jars   14, 15

L

leaves   6
limited palette   13

M

marker pen   8, 14, 15

O

origami   20, 21, 23

P

pattern   5, 7, 10, 11, 19, 22
pebbles   7, 10, 22
pencil   7, 8, 12, 21, 22
permanent fabric marker pen   9, 12
permanent marker   7, 14

R

rafia   14, 15
rough sketch   12, 23

S

shading   19
shell   7
sketch   10, 16
sketchbook   5, 9
steampunk   16, 23

T

technique   5, 23
three dimensions   6, 23
thumbnail sketch   18, 23
tone   7
tracing   12, 18
T-shirt   12, 13, 22

Z

zig-zag   11, 14, 22